C000245460

ABOUT THE AUTHOR

Luke Wright is a poet and broadcaster. His poetry stage shows have toured the world and played sold-out runs in London and Edinburgh. He is a regular contributor to BBC Radio and his verse documentary on Channel 4 was nominated for a Grierson Award. His first collection, *Mondeo Man*, was published in 2013.

PRAISE FOR WHAT I LEARNED FROM JOHNNY BEVAN

The Scotsman Fringe First Award, 2015
The Stage Awards for Acting Excellence 2015

'Pulsating, neatly handled piece of poetic storytelling … the breakneck storytelling is clear and gives Wright's seething, dynamic poetry the room it needs to motor.'
★ ★ ★ ★ Lyn Gardner, *The Guardian*

'This is such a rich piece of writing. There's so much in it. It's resonant and timely and it tells a story compellingly. […] It says so much about idealism and youth and maturity and compromise – and love – and the places life can take you, the incremental sneaky way that years have, of passing'
★ ★ ★ ★ ★ Natasha Tripney, *Exeunt Magazine*

'Performed in verse that bounds and soars effortlessly … Taking in issues of class, privilege and the death of Labour, *What I Learned from Johnny Bevan* is a compelling and relatable exploration of growing up and facing hard truths'
★ ★ ★ ★ ★ Cat Acheson, *The Skinny*

ALSO BY LUKE WRIGHT

POETRY

Mondeo Man (Penned in the Margins, 2013)

The Vile Ascent Of Lucien Gore And What The People Did (Nasty
   Little Press, 2011)

High Performance (Nasty Little Press, 2009)

NON-FICTION

Who Writes This Crap? with Joel Stickley (Penguin, 2007)

What I Learned from Johnny Bevan

Luke Wright

For Caitlyn,

[signature]

Penned in the Margins

LONDON

PUBLISHED BY PENNED IN THE MARGINS
Toynbee Studios, 28 Commercial Street, London E1 6AB
www.pennedinthemargins.co.uk

First published 2016

Printed in the United Kingdom by TJ International

ISBN
978-1908058331

THANKS

I would like to thank Tom Chivers at Penned in the Margins for giving this play the chance to live on as a book.

Thanks also to everyone who worked on the original show with me: Ian Catskilkin, Tom Clutterbuck, Steve Forster, Kate Harvey, Paul Jellis, Pasco Q Kevlin and Sam Ratcliffe.

I would like to thank Norwich Arts Centre and Writers' Centre Norwich for co-commissioning the piece, and the wonderful, vital Arts Council England for their additional financial support. Thanks also to all at Summerhall, who gave me a home at the 2015 Edinburgh Festival Fringe.

Special thanks to Tim Clare, Molly Naylor and Joel Stickley, all of whom gave me excellent early feedback on the script.

Extra special thanks to Joe Luke Murphy who acted as dramaturg and script editor — your editorial zings made this double good.

And, as always, my love and deepest gratitude to my family — Sally, Aidan and Sam.

For P.

What I Learned from Johnny Bevan

To London then, that fatted beast
on which the whole world comes to feast,
all private woe and public farce;
where money twerks its oiled arse
in gorgeous, fenced-off Georgian squares
and starchy oligarchical lairs;
where soaring, steel-glass towers sit
in ancient, ghoulish, plague-filled pits;
where gap-toothed roads left by the Blitz
are soaked in years of pigeon shit;
where listless folk roam airless malls
as slaves to airbrushed siren calls
then, gobsmacked, flash their plastic cash
and fill their hearts and lungs with ash;
where policy is signed and sealed
then forced upon the shires and fields;
where money men spin even more
from love of it and fear of war
(like bookie blokes they will their stocks
as food bank queues ring grotty blocks);
where cut-glass vowels meet glottal stops;
where half-cut kids in chicken shops
dream dreams as false as talent shows,
these rebels wrapped in branded clothes,
this lunar race illuminated

by their screens but never sated,
all within their reach at last
but safe behind the steel-laced glass —
it's oh so close but out of touch,
it's not for you, they know that much,
it's not for you, it's not for you,
it's not for you...
                    to London then.

To REGENT STREET, a throng of culture hacks:
those blokes, too old for Converse, wearing Converse,
sucking vapes. All mid-life paunch, Fred Perrys
bit too tight with branded record bags.
And me. I'm Nick. I'm one of them. Oh yeah,
despite the baby face it should be clear
the sheen of youth has long since left my chops.
Too many sea-eyed nights and almost-truths.
We scan our phones: some distant Facebook friend,
her profile pic a chubby, grinning kid,
complains: *My little monster cried all night!*
I don't have a monster. Something else,
some other creeping thing, keeps me awake.
I'm knackered and I don't want to be here.
The launch of yet another festival,
a playground for the bankers of tomorrow
to drink their fill of glossy counter-culture
like Tuborg from the branded plastic cup.

"Hello, hello, hello, right everyone."
A woman, early twenties, megaphone.
"Right, welcome everybody, in a moment
the coaches will depart and take us to
URBANIA..." A pause, she scans her notes.
"The brand new urban festival for London!"

Urbania had built-up quite a buzz.
The promise of a weekend festival
without the mud. The latest edgy acts
at a secret location in the city.
Secret, that is, that *was*, until today.
Today the secret venue is made public,
the acts will be announced and tickets sold.
Today the likes of me and all these guys
will get to walk the site and hear the spin
so we can start our routine work of flogging
this brand new jewel in British culture's crown.
We board the coach and start a slow shunt east.

§

The coach is abuzz with the gobshiting natter
of fifty-five journos and not enough clues.
Locations and line-ups proposed and then shot down;
conjecture and wish lists served up like they're news.

And bang in the centre of all of the gossip,
a brace of young publicists: Tilly and Milly.
Yes, you know the type I mean, all posh and glossy,
part pushy, part flirty and pleasantly silly.

From Pinner or somewhere where mum and dad keep them
while Tilly or Milly intern in the sprawl
for travel cards, samplers, guest lists and freebies.
And maybe a job at the end of it all.

And this is their moment: fronting Urbania.
They coax, hint and wink with some well-rehearsed titters.
Peculiar choices for *edgy* and *urban*.
Think Duchess of Cornwall, but better at Twitter.

§

This used to be the sort thing I thrived on;
in the know, the skinny on my lips.
Affected nonchalance to hide the fact
my heart was singing out to write reviews,
to meet my heroes: bands and writers who'd
reveal some erstwhile unreported fact
to me; to help great novels find their readers;
to shape the narratives of rock 'n' roll.
It blew my socks off, claimed my aching heart.
On junkets like this, I would feel so lucky.
And then... it never happens in a moment.
Love doesn't die in battlefield glory,
just slinks away one evening through the tunnel

it's secretly been chipping at for years
until, next day, you've just an empty room,
a makeshift shovel lying on the floor.

§

"So Nick, darling, Nick, Nick," (it's Tilly — no *Milly*)
"Nick babes, you know, don't you? Come on, you do!"
I proffer a watery grin, put my hands up,
a shrug and a faux-friendly *haven't a clue.*

"Well, I know that you know our literary headliner.
Good mate of yours from your Guardian stint..."
And really I do know. It's Jonathan Tyle.
I play Milly's game with a good-natured wink.

Oh Jonathan Tyle, Jonathan Tyle,
the whole world's gone mental for Jonathan Tyle.
They're hooked on his sneering and withering similes;
they're desperate to favourite and rent out his bile.

Oh Jonathan Tyle, the scourge of celebrity
who snapped at the ankles of power and spin,
then got his own telly show, married a model
and spread out his work till it was Rizla-thin.

And maybe it's Jonathan Tyle that's the problem
and, no, not, as some think, because I am jealous,
but rather that I help promote these pretenders
then airbrush the anger and smooth out the menace.

I want to believe in the art and ideas
in a world where the author's name dwarfs the book's title.
Like never before I need it to change me,
and everything's quite good, but nothing is vital.

"Don't you dare tweet that." She smiles as she gets up.
I waggle my iPhone and she looks delighted.
Of course I'm not jealous of Jonathan Tyle.
I'm jealous of Milly — because she's excited.

§

The coach is pounding down the A13
when branded info sheets are handed round.
Urbania is more than just the music.
Urbania is issues and debate.
Hear talks on tackling austerity.
Book your bijou weekend chalet now!
And just as I emit a raspy sigh
the bus pulls left and Milly coos: "We're here!"

And from the rain-flecked window I can see
four high-rise tower blocks, their water-stained,
grey concrete looming down upon the coach.
There's something so familiar in the walkways;
it's dizzy *déjà-vu* as we file off.
"This," Tilly gestures at the tower blocks,
"was once The Grooms, an infamous estate."
She steps towards our little huddled group,
recounting riots, rapes and gangland murders
excitedly while cribbing from her notes.
"Forget the parks and meadowlands and mud."
(She's reading now.) "Urbania is different!
Long abandoned The Grooms provides a bold
Dystopian setting for our festival..."
But I can't hear her now. My head is spinning.
The grotty tower blocks are dancing round me.
The Grooms... The Grooms... The Grooms... I know this place.
The very words light corners of my mind;
great grizzly hands are groping in my guts
and churning up the murk and guilt and fear.
The Grooms... The Grooms... The Grooms... I knows this place.
Some eighteen years ago I stood right here
with Johnny Bevan. This was Johnny's home.

PINT OF PAST MATE? Drink that dram!
Look, the world's been Instagrammed!
The Grooms is washed in orangeade.
A honied hum, a lush aubade,
gives shape to late, late August dawn.
Two stick-thin lads sat shooting scorn,
high on a fifteen-storey roof,
in tatty, plaid-grey Camden suits,
a crushed tin nest of Red Stripe cans
around their boots — they're making plans.
"You gotta do it, Nick, you gotta.
Novels: mate, that's fucking proper.
I'll put you on the reading list.
A fucking Whitehall initiative."
He's standing now, half silhouetted
by the rising sun, and says it
with his usual cheeky point.
He grins, he nabs the other's joint.
He breathes it deep, and kneads his hair:
"I tell you, Nick, mate, Tony Blair's
all right. I mean, he's on the case,
but he's not from this sort of place.
And that," he booms in mock-decree,
"*Is why this crumbling isle needs me*."
He sucks more smoke in, grimaces,

then flicks the dog-end off the edge.
They watch it spin and spin and spin
and spin until it vanishes...

§

Eleven months before that roof-top scene,
my lanky frame was hunched up in the back.
My mum clicked knitting needles in the front.
And everything dad said was tin on glass.
A steady trill of things like *digs* and *dons*
as if he'd cast me as the hero in
a jaunty, puffed-up Sixties campus novel.
Sure, he was excited for me, but
his speech was trampling on my new life.
"When I was there... I bet it hasn't changed...
A brilliant pub... Now what's it called again?
The Flag, I think. Good, student-friendly place..."
I squirmed and mouthed a silent *Fucking Clearing!*
To wind up at my father's alma mater!
Three years of walking where my father walked,
of drinking where he drank, the same old japes.
My dad had eulogised his uni days
ad nauseam since I was nine or ten.
"The best days of your life, the best friends too!"

Which only served to highlight what I saw
in him; that adulthood was all downhill
from there. I didn't want to be my dad.
A small town lawyer, bored and tired by work.
Christ, the way he'd sigh when he got home.
I wanted desperately to do my own thing.
But there I was. I'd wanted to do English.
But dad had scared me off. "Law sets you up.
I know you, Nick. You'll want to have nice things.
Just get your law degree. A safety net."

§

Hugs and tears and *I'll be fines*
then I became The Student.
My room was compact, worn and frayed,
but still a big improvement.

I made myself a cup of tea,
I chose a favourite tune,
then lay down on the narrow bed
to seize the afternoon.

For all my cringing at my Dad
I'd sat and listened too.

The best friends that you'll ever make:
that needed to be true.

I'd had mates back in Colchester.
I'd even kissed some girls.
But nobody I'd ever met
was really from my world.

They were cars and football clubs
or make-up and TV.
I was books, I was music,
I was poetry

and lyrics scrawled on army bags
and looking for 'a scene' —
and if that sounds pretentious,
it is: I'm eighteen!

Now with my old life left behind
I couldn't wait to start
on gin-soaked existential talk
and afternoons of art.

Yeah, that, and probably get an ear-ring.
God! I was excited!

I'd never have to fake support for
Colchester United!

My future friends were scarves and bikes,
old books stacked on their racks,
all baccy tins and *Ban the Bomb*
and vintage leather macs

and turtle-necks and berets...
Well, I wasn't really certain.
But still the stage was set; now
it was time to raise the curtain.

So off the bed, kitchen-bound
in search of future friends,
arms laden with the Argos pans
mum bought me last weekend.

My belly full of drunken moths,
I backed into the door,
the pots secured beneath my chin.
I turned around and saw

these nine lads holding Fosters tins,
all football shirts and spots.

In lad-salute I raised my chin
and fucking dropped the pots!

Clatter! Blush! And *fuck me mate*.
I scrabbled on the floor
in strip-light hum. Looked up, then grimaced:
"Hi. Nick. Doing Law..."

"All right mate. Y'all right mate.
All right mate. All right
All right mate. Y'all right mate.
All right mate. All right."

The final lad stepped forward smiling,
grabbed a fallen pan.
"You all right Nick? I'm Simon, mate.
Harsh luck. You want a can?

Hey! The Argos student starter kit!
Same one my mum bought."
He handed me a lukewarm beer.
"So who do you support?"

§

And so the grand adventure came
in laddish, lagered haze
with cheesy student disco nights
and sluggish, sleepy days.

My dad was right, of course. Of course!
Law was loads of work.
I'd sleepwalk through my seminars
then don a smartish shirt

and head out with my flatmates
to the shabby student bar,
play pool (which I was rubbish at),
talk football, clubs and cars.

And birds. Yes, every part of their
anatomy was riffed on.
And it was harmless, generally,
but Christ, just like my sixth form!

§

On bonfire night we're down the pub;
there's football on the screen.
It's Scary Al's lot, Sunderland,

v Tottenham, Simon's team.

It's good 'n' all. It's stoppage time
and then a penalty,
which means that Spurs could win the match:
a glorious 4-3.

Al's gelled head was in his hands:
"No way! I feel sick!"
The ball was placed, the run began,
but just before the kick

the TV screen went blank: "You what!?
Oi, fucking turn it on."
An awkward looking boy stepped up.
"Oh, hello everyone.

The Lit Soc's weekly open mic
will start just after eight."
"Give a fuck! Just turn it on
before I lamp you mate."

"Oh. Righto. Sorry. Which one is it?"
He gauchely groped the box.
Eventually the screen lit up.

And Sunderland had lost.

With scattered coughs of *Wanker! Tosser!*
aimed at Lit Soc's crew,
we all drank up, teased Scary Al,
and weighed up what to do.

"The Lit Soc Open Mic? Do one."
Plans were duly made.
We drained our dregs and stood just as
the first act took the stage.

"Oh Gentlemen, you break my heart!"
We turned, and taunting us,
a skinny lad in ice-blue jeans,
Fred Perry buttoned-up.

In scuffed-up, shin-high, black DMs
he gripped the microphone;
half bow, half snarl, he winked at us.
"That's right boys, you go home."

With muffled *Twat* they exited,
but I was rooted there.
A crowd of twenty students but

this fella didn't care.

He prowled around the tiny stage
like it was Glastonbury,
all boyish charm and lupine grist.
"Right! Time for poetry!

This one's about the government.
I'll go out on a limb;
I decided to forgive the swines."
Then words spilled out of him.

> *Now, I've been known to say some nasty things about the Tories;*
> *I've cast them as the villains in a slew of foul-mouthed stories.*
> *I've painted bar rooms blue with lewd descriptions of their mums;*
> *Lamonted them and caused a Major ball ache with my puns.*
>
> *But older, wiser, richer now, I'm taken by their verve,*
> *and with my ratty council flat, I've so much to conserve.*
> *Oh thank you Mr Lilley sir, a pittance just for me?*
> *I want to thank the bally lot and have them round for tea!*
>
> *Imagine them all sipping coyly!*
> *Come on Norman, grab a doily.*
> *Mike, they lied, you're not so oily.*

I wanna take tea with the Tories.

Flogging peasants? What a slog!
Here, put your feet up on the dog.
Howard, Heseltine and Hogg!
I wanna take tea with the Tories.

A wash of grey throughout my hovel;
stiffly perched they slurp and gobble.
Archer! Bore us with your novel!
I wanna take tea with the Tories.

Shoes off, Ken. Hate to ask,
but you've trampled in some working class.
Mr Mellor, have a tart!
I wanna take tea with the Tories.

Alistair! Good Lad! Brought your whip!
Someone fetch her from the crypt.
We warned these rebels Ma is strict.
I wanna take tea with the Tories.

Tarzan, darling, love the hair;
Virginia, park your derrière;
Mr Redwood, please don't stare;

I wanna take tea with the Tories.

Ah, Master Hague, your mother too.
Hello! hello! Pull up a pew!
I think we have some juice for you!
I wanna take tea with the Tories.

A slew of sleaze and union flags,
air thick with fart and classist gags.
Brown envelopes for party bags!
I wanna take tea with the Tories.

I wanna take tea with the Tories;
and when it's getting late
I'll send the hoary bastards out
to walk through my estate.

Sorry fellas, street light's fucked.
Cuts I think, what rotten luck.
Mind the dog shit, human piss;
I know, how can we live like this?
Oh careful now, those lads have knives.
Quick, the cars, run for your lives!
One of them's stood on your bonnet.
Should it have more wheels on it?

I think it might need those to work.
Oh! No way out! Ah this might hurt.
Sorry, nothing I can do!
Oh fancy that, your blood's not blue!
Oh dear! Oh dear! Oh what a mess.
Thanks for coming. All the best!

And after all that frothing bile,
a sweet, lopsided grin;
he brushed his messy curls away
and looked so genuine.

We whooped and clapped. He stooped and bowed.
"Thanks. You lot were good!
And my name's Johnny Bevan. Don't forget it."
I never would.

§

I looked around and saw my mates had gone.
Johnny Bevan was leant against the bar
as poet after poet took the stage.
I studied him; somehow I couldn't picture
Johnny on a bike or in a scarf,

but I was sure that right there stood the friend
I'd waited all my safe and boring life
to meet. Yes, Johnny Bevan was the one.

"I really loved your poem man.
Like, how do you remember it all...
But like seriously, your memory's amazing...
Not just your memory...
The words as well.
I mean you're not a elephant, are you...?
Cos, cos, they've got really good memories, haven't they?
I mean, I've always wondered, like, how do they, like, know elephants
have got really good memories?
I'm not asking you, I'm just, y'know.
Anyway, that...
Can I get you a pint?
A pint of rum and coke?
Oh right, a rum a coke.
Yeah, cool. Coming up."

And *oh* the cringe. The awful, awful cringe.
I kicked myself and ordered up the drinks.
"Thanks fella." Johnny smiled and raised his glass.
Beneath his cork-screw hair, these grass-green eyes
that seemed to ache and sparkle all at once.

I just assumed he'd go and find his friends,
but Johnny stayed and sipped the rum and coke.
An easy silence fell upon us both.
Then Johnny turned to me and it began:
all literature and politics and bands.
The Pistols. Scargill. Thatcher. Smiths. The Fall.
A tapestry of British life spilled out.
Each sentence like a grainy TV screen
with some defining moment of our time.
Nye Bevan. Richey Manic. Morrissey.
Black Adder. Miners. Churchill. Kinnock. Blair.
The Pythons. Peter Cook. Yes! Derek and Clive!
All laced with *cunts* and *fucks* and *twats* and *proper*.
That was Johnny's favourite. *Proper. Proper.*
"There ain't no middle ground: it's shit or proper."
What's more, the bloke was right. I rode each wave
of Johnny's diatribe a constant *YES!*
All *yes* and *yup* and *totally* and *bang on*.
He span my wooden answers into gold
then crashed down on his syllables again.
He slurred and ranted, whispered, joked and trilled.
Each word performed like he was still on stage:
alliteration, crackle, spit and wit.
His voice a patchwork quilt of dialects,
a smash of London consonants and vowels

all jostling with the argot of the posh,
exaggerated barrow boy meets toff;
from Churchill into Lydon over Cleese,
each brief impression bleeding on the last;
a clanking, choral symphony of Britain.

Till time was called and strip light broke the mood.
Then, pissed and happy, me and Johnny stumbled
back across the campus to our halls.
"So you live in the posh halls, do ya Nick?"
Right then? Was that the first? The pampered pang.
That sense of guilt I've come to know and loathe.
I've learned to hide it too, but way back then
my silence must have spilled my guts for me,
cos Johnny gripped my shoulder: "Come on mate!
Chin up — don't hate the finer things in life.
Just blame the swines in charge who hand it out.
We'll bludgeon them and build new halls for all!"
He coughed and spluttered. "Fuck's sake Nick, I'm pissed.
It's been a laugh. Let's do it all again.
Adieu, old boy. Well met." Then he was gone.

§

November and December blurred
as Johnny's rant went on
across a score of magic evenings
soaked in verse and rum;

in dim-lit student kitchenettes
where cheesy-pasta dried,
where threads of baccy garnished plates,
where adolescence died.

I left the lads with the shirts and lager
shouting at the screen
to bellyache with Johnny
over lentil-based cuisine.

His little group of punks and mods
showed me a brave new world
of Nestlé boycotts, Chomsky, Marx
and, crucially, some girls.

Rach was badges, back-combed hair
and army surplus gear,
a voice like late-night radio
and armed with quotes from Greer.

Johnny rarely stopped his spiel
but Rach could do the job.
"Johnny, love, we know, you've told us!
Fookin' shut yer gob."

Though she was one to talk, and talk.
In fact the whole lot were:
Byron, Michael, Susan, Lou,
a charged, excited burr.

And then next day I'd bunk my lectures,
plug gaps in my knowledge
with library books and Johnny's tapes.
I'd wasted sixth form college,

I wouldn't waste this chance, I thought.
My friends became my home
and by the dark days down to Christmas
I could hold my own.

§

But I loved Johnny best of all;
our back-and-forth just sung.
I told him all about my dad;

he talked about his mum.

"She's proper, Nick. She brought me up.
I never knew my dad.
Nah, no big thing. He's well fucked off;
it doesn't make me sad.

She's great and now she's shot of Keith...
step-dad, since I was ten.
He fucking... well, it doesn't matter,
won't see him again.

Look Nick, your dad seems all right.
Sure he sounds annoying
but that, mate, ain't the issue here.
The problem you're avoiding

is you don't want to be a lawyer...
SO DON'T DO LAW, YOU TWAT!
Switch to English Literature.
He'll be all right with that."

§

And so at last to 1997.
Well-shot of law, I lost whole afternoons
immersed in Modernism: Mansfield, Joyce and Woolf.
All soundtracked by the skaggy krautrock drone
of 'Beetlebum', the death of jaunty Britpop.
"I know they sound like yanks, but this is proper."
And Geri wore *that dress* and Britain held
its breath to wait for Tony Blair and Labour.

I became obsessed with politics.
My parents always 'exercise their right'
but issues and debate are not their thing.
My mum, she has this motto: "In polite
society one never talks about
three things: religion, race and politics."
I told my new friends this one smoke-filled evening.
Johnny grinned and quipped, "She left out fisting,"
and fired off his cod-Sid James guffaw.
The very thought of not discussing things
was alien to Johnny and the rest.
And he and Byron, Rach and me all joined
the Labour Party, went out leafleting.
"I remember '92," said Johnny.
"My mum and me stayed up. Christ, she was gutted.
I sort of understood, knew it was bad.

Then Keith came back, all pissed up, fucking...
But things are different now, eh? Sure, Blair's smarmy;
lawyer in't he? Nick, what might have been!
But he's a clever bloke, they're playing it safe.
They'll win, and then they'll shift it to the left.
Shit, I'm buzzing." I was buzzing too.
I'd only just discovered this oppression!
The miner's strikes and poll tax in one go.
But still, a month or two of right-wing rule
seemed long enough to me. And though I'd never
seen my dad on picket lines like Michael
or survived on dole like Lou and Johnny,
I, like every doe-eyed student try-hard,
felt my cause in every aching fibre.

§

And so to May 1st and Dimbleby
and Peter Snow's Swingometer of change.
My telly meant my little room was rammed.
The cabin bed took five, all feet up, fags lit,
while Johnny paced, impersonated, swore
and laughed the balmy late-Spring night away.
Midnight past and Edgbaston went red.
We cheered and whooped and clumsily slapped hands.

Then Basildon. "God bless the Essex Man."
As all around the country Tories fell:
Forsyth and Rifkind, Rumbold, Currie, Laing.
And then Portillo. "Go on Enfield. Yes!"
"Poor love," said Rach, "I almost feel sorry...
Nah. Fuck him, homophobic Tory bastard."
When Bell took Tatton from Neil Hamilton
it felt so sweet to see his crumpled face.
I revelled in that tribal *schadenfreude*,
the sweaty hugs and whoops of base elation.
A total letting go. I'd found my folk
and here we were, a boozy sweat of smoke
and hope — and on the cusp of something new.
The Blairs appeared like white-toothed royalty,
a bulb pop of celebrity and power.
I held my breath with wowed intoxication.
Tony grinned. "It's looking pretty good."
And yes, it did. It looked so very good.
Majority achieved and my room span,
all lager, brandy baccy, spit and tears,
the tiny telly drowned by tunes and cries of:
"Turn it up! I don't want to hear D:REAM!"

§

Time smeared like grease across the lens of morning
till I found Johnny dancing on his own;
a strange, lop-sided, tip-toed waltz across
the roof outside his poxy student room.
When he saw me he kicked his empty bottle
off the roof; it hit the grass below
but somehow didn't smash. "*I love you Nicky!*
And if it's quite all right, let's have a quickie,
blah blah blah blah blah, blah blah blah blah blah..."
He clamped his elbow round my neck and kissed
my cheek. Then, holding me at arm's length, seemed
to breathe me in. His grass-green eyes all bloodshot.
"My God, it's been a fucking long time coming!
This is it. This country's gonna change.
Oh Nick, mate. Fucking yes. We bloody did it."
We sat sweat-backed against his bedroom window,
staring at the silver mists that hung
above the grass; each breath a hopeful cloud.
"Here, Nick, mate. Come and stay with me this summer.
See the Grooms, before they blow it up.
They're bound to build much better council houses.
What's that word they use. They'll ... gentrify us!"
He slurred a Churchill: "I shall be a gent!"
I grinned. "I'd love to mate, I'd really love to."
My green green heart a thump of love and hope.

"I T'S TRAIN OR TUBE and then a bus
      but I prefer to walk" —
      and so we did, with backpacks on,
the effort numbed by talk

and cheeky nips of hip-flask rum;
past chicken and kebab shops,
a hundred shabby newsagents
and tags all over bus stops

and Greengrocers with foreign veg,
these things I'd never seen.
"That's plantain not bananas, twat.
My God, you're fucking green.

Although, right now, I bet you're feeling
really rather white."
I pulled my best *whatever* face
but knew that he was right.

I'd been to London loads before
but never parts like this,
a stretch outside my comfort zone
and Johnny ripped the piss

till I confessed the only black friends
I had ever had
were Byron back at uni and
this work mate of my dad's.

"Well he don't count, dick!" Johnny laughed.
He punched me on the shoulder.
"There were only two black kids at my school
and both of them were older."

"Jesus Christ, you're from the fifties!"
"I can't help that, though.
I'm not a racist, Johnny."
"For fuck's sake Nick, I know.

You can't change where you come from mate.
And on that sombre note:
behold The Grooms Estate, my friend.
That's where you spent your vote."

§

The towers grew from Johnny's outstretched hand:
window upon window upon window
clad drearily in pebble-dashed, beige stucco.

Four chubby fingers jabbing at the clouds.
The sheer scale took my breath: the length of pipes
that scored each tower's face; the symmetry
of staircase upon staircase upon staircase;
the tiny dot of someone on a landing
far, far above our heads, ten storeys high.
I couldn't picture either of my parents
even visiting a place like this.
It made me think of photoshoots and bands.
It felt so urban. "Johnny, mate, it's cool."
"I knew you'd think that, Nick. It's fucking skuzz.
The lifts don't work. The whole place stinks of piss.
There's needles in stairwells. Murders happen."
"I just mean, like the style, it's Modernist."
"Well durr, that's why they built them, innit, twat,
some clever-clever German cunt or something
wanking over straight clean lines and stacking
human beings up in boxes. Guess what?
Human beings don't like being stacked
in boxes. Human beings fucking hate it.
Especially if none of them have jobs.
The Grooms ain't fucking cool, Nick, it's depressing."
Johnny stopped and grinned. "Although," he giggled,
putting on a Sybil Fawlty smarm,
"We do so hope that you enjoy your stay."

And in the warmth of sun and rum and youth
our laughter quickly turned to gasped hysterics.

§

Sandra Bevan had his eyes,
the aching grass-green spark.
She worked shifts at a factory,
left while it was dark

and came back in at 3pm,
the same time me and Johnny
surfaced after boozy nights
in pants and t-shirts, groggy

and in need of well-brewed tea,
the only sort she made.
We'd take it in her retro lounge
and talk while Johnny played

his tapes or read us things from books.
I loved the way she spoke:
expressive, Cockney, mumsy too,
a voice like coal and soap.

She'd swear as well, and let us smoke,
so unlike any parent
that I'd ever met before;
she treated us like adults.

And Johnny loved to make a fuss.
"Here, put your feet up, mum.
I'll whip you up a omelette, yeah?
You want a nip of rum?"

Then, after tea, a drink or two,
we left her to her soaps
and headed to the boozer,
scored some weed, then sat and smoked

on some grass bank or other
in the muggy summer haze
and built our futures out of blarney,
slowly stacked the days

until the days had turned to weeks
and summertime had frayed.
And as the evenings fell away
Johnny's banter swayed

increasingly to politics;
he was obsessed with Labour.
His rants became more serious.
Before, when he'd have made a

gag about a politician,
now he'd grab a book
and quote great chunks of text at me.
"You see, that proves it, look!"

His future lay in politics
and all else had to go:
"I can't be arsed with poetry,
I can't be arsed with show,

I know it might be sophomoric,
naivety and hope,
but someone's gotta change the world.
I'm gonna be that bloke."

And I told Johnny my ambitions,
showed him clunky prose,
the stuttered starts of shonky stories.
Johnny always chose

the choicest bits. He'd clap his hands
and read the line out loud.
"That's fucking great, you nailed it Nick!"
It guess it made me proud.

I knew that he was being kind.
I knew the stuff was pap.
But when I'd wake up next day,
foggy headed, feeling crap,

Johnny's slurred encouragements
came back to me again
and more and more I found myself
reaching for a pen.

And so to late, late August dawn;
two stick thin lads sat shooting scorn,
high on a fifteen-storey roof,
in tatty, plaid-grey Camden suits...

He sucks the smoke in, grimaces,
then flicks the dog-end off the edge;
they watch it spin and spin and spin
and spin until it vanishes.

Till eight o'clock and back to Johnny's mum's;
we traipsed up fourteen flights of pissy stairs
with ashtray mouths and heavy, bandy legs,
our minds a quiet hum, our hearts content.
"That's not like mum, she never leaves the lights on.
Door's unlocked." He called into the flat.
"Mum? Mum, are you still here? You all right?"
He threw his jacket down and called again.
I came into the room behind him slowly.
I saw him first. Sat in the corner. Keith.
He watched us from semi-shadow. "Johnny..."
He turned and saw him sat there. "What the fuck?"
Johnny was shaking, lip curled, eyes welled-up.
"She doesn't want you, *we* don't want you here."
Then bang on cue she came in, things exploded.
Sandra and I thrust between the two
in clouds of tears and insults. Keith was yelling:
"You think you know it all, hey, don't ya Johnny?
You think you've got this whole world fucking sussed.
Well, what would you know, boy? Huh? You don't know.
This life will grind you down, you'll fuck it up
the same as me, the same as..." Johnny threw
an ashtray; it flew just past Keith's right ear
and hit the wall, a shock and smash of glass.
Keith shot across the room, left jab to Johnny's

jaw. He split his lip wide open. Blood poured
down his chin and neck. "You fucking cunt."
He swung for him and missed. "I'll fucking kill you."
Keith stood tall, a grizzly puff of chest,
as Sandra begged and prised the men apart.
Her husband kicked the wall; her son collapsed
into a chair and wept. He looked so young.
His grass-eyes dull, his chin a claret mess.
"Nick. Nick, love." Sandra's voice was barely there.
"You'll have go, just leave us. Please. Just go."
I swallowed hard, I couldn't fucking move.
"Johnny... mate... please Johnny... Johnny... come..."
But Johnny Bevan wouldn't look at me.
He spat blood on the carpet. "Nick, just go."

"SO HERE WE HAVE our bijou weekend chalets.
The north tower is for VIPs and artists.
The south is for, ah, media and staff.
The east and west for hire. As well as yurts
and bell tents on *The Rec* between the blocks."
Tilly flicks a switch, the flat lights up.
"It's all mod cons, of course: 4K TV,
Nespresso and Egyptian cotton bedding.
But don't be tempted by an early night;
we've DJs on till five." A short, meek laugh.
She almost turns to leave, then stops: "Oh yeah,
each chalet boasts a range of photographs
by cutting-edge photographer Peter Daley.
They show the harsh realities of life
before The Grooms was gentrified by us."
She gestures at a framed, high-contrast snap;
a monochrome of kids on the estate.
They stand and smoke. There's litter at their feet.
"And prints of Peter's gritty work will be
available to purchase from our shop."

AS JAUNDICED NIPS of early Autumn
came to rural Essex
I called and called and called my friend,
sent a couple of letters

but only got a postcard back,
unsigned; a single line
in Johnny's rushed and jagged hand.
Don't worry Nick, I'm fine.

And that's the way he played it
when the term began again,
the same impersonations,
the usual verbal gems.

We barely talked about that morning.
"Don't tell no one else.
Just leave it Nick, it doesn't matter,
keep it to yourself.

I'm never going back again.
If she wants him, that's fine.
Let him piss her life away;
the cunt ain't touching mine."

But when the group went down the pub
or met up after class,
Johnny never came along.
"You go, I can't be arsed."

We'd find him in the kitchen later,
maudlin, frustrated,
slurring bits of textbooks at us,
getting irritated

if anybody missed his point.
"You lot are fucking thick!"
And week on week these bitter rants
replaced the playful schtick.

And when he stormed off to his bedroom
we were glad of it.
"Fucking hell, mate, I'm too stressed
to deal with Johnny's shit."

I joined the student paper,
wrote reviews of books and bands,
and stay up late with other people;
ranting, making plans

and living life liked Johnny showed me,
angry with the friend
I figured just got bored of me,
no empathy back then.

Till on the fridge in jagged script
we found a note one day.
Adieu. I've gone to join the world.
Stay Greasy. X X J.

§

And sure, I'd like to say I searched for Johnny.
But I didn't. Life got in the way.
Besides, I felt like he'd abandoned me.
I moved to London, wrote for magazines:
The NME, The Guardian, The Times.
I lived the London life; a layer cake
of gigs and sex and arthouse cinemas,
never more than fifteen feet away
from a DJ. My twenties swallowed, wincing
like tequila. Shot glass slammed back down.
The same the same the same the same again.
Five years became ten years and then fifteen.
The Dome, No Logo, Napster, Doctor Who,

Guantánamo, The God Delusion, Twitter,
Big Brother, New Orleans, The Libertines,
The Office, 9/11, David Cameron.
But sometimes on the night bus home, I'd stop.
"Is that him? Nah, he's too short... wrong hair..."
I'd spend these sad fluorescent journeys home
awash with narratives that numbed my guilt.
Until, one Thursday morning, Rachel called.
"It's Johnny, Nick. I've found him, he's on Facebook.
He's living in a squat... in Colchester.
I know... You gotta see his profile, Nick."
His statuses were regular and FUCK-laced,
often CAPS LOCKED, full of bile, and yet
it wasn't quite the Johnny I had known.
I lost a morning trawling through his life,
all clicked detective work. It wasn't hard
to piece together. Johnny wasn't shy.
He'd fought and lost a local council seat.
That must have been '01; his hair all neat,
he stood there beaming in a red rosette.
But after that the love affair with Labour
soured. *Class Traitors! Tory Lite! War Crimes!*
They've sold us off and out. They've kept us down!
Blunt invective interspersed with photos;
a hundred marches, demos, rallies, protests:

Gleneagles, May Day, IMF, Iraq.

He marched against austerity and cuts.

He marched for teachers, nurses, fire fighters,

Gaza, Lebanon, Afghanistan.

His hair grew long, cropped short, then long again;

his grass-green eyes grew resolute and distant;

his statuses more cynical and hard.

He cheered the downfall of his former party:

Serves them right, and now look what we got!

The articles he shared both left and right,

but always partisan, acerbic, sharp.

There ain't no middle ground. It's shit or proper.

Christ though, some of it was proper bleak.

Screenloads and loads of unrelenting comment,

pugilistic prose and discontent,

increasingly with nationalistic bent.

At least this lot address the working class!

And though it seemed a contradictory mess,

it somehow formed one picture; it made sense.

But fucking hell, it's just, he seemed so sad.

And all my love for him came rushing back.

I clicked the message button: *Hello Johnny.*

§

I knew his building, not far from my uncle's.
My mother used to rush me past the place.
She'd tut and hurry on: *unsavoury.*
Detached and overgrown with creeping plants,
Victorian brickwork showing here and there.
It had, at some point, been a grand old place.
But now the front garden was wild and fly-tipped.
The large bay windows boarded up, the sills
half-crumbled off, the bricked front steps come loose,
and great flakes of black paint hanging from the door.
I rapped it hard. No answer. Then again.
Till finally a clatter, dim expletives.
"All right. All right. For fuck's sake Nick, you're keen."
And there my old friend stood. Still whippet thin.
The cheek bones just a touch less angular.
"Jesus Christ! Is that a fucking top-knot?
You dick." He shook his head. "Well come on then."
We went into the front room: folding chair,
a mattress on the floor, a slew of books
beside the pillow: Orwell, Marx and Steyn.
"I know why Rach has sent you here. That stuff
on Facebook. Europe stuff. Them articles."
Johnny pulled his hand back to his forehead.
"Oh Nick, I bring grave news. It's Johnny Bevan!
What! Not Johnny. Yes Nick, he's... a racist.

A racist?! That's the worst -ist you can be!
I'm right though aren't I Nick? That's what you think."
"You're sharing things supporting bloody UKIP!
That's not us, we don't believe in that."
"Perhaps *we* don't, but you don't speak for me.
We haven't said a word in fifteen years;
you can't presume they've treated us the same.
How you gonna vote? For Miliband?
Pathetic. Nick, don't fall for it again!
The Labour Party's over. They left us!
And no it's not just Tony's crap crusade.
Fuck Iraq! Well they already did.
But fuck it, that's some other cunt's betrayal.
They always make out that's the worst he did.
Well, what about Academies? Clause 4?
The market? Fucking PFI in everything!
Oh, *we're the party of the NHS,*
they cry so piously these days but they
began foundation trusts. And killed our grants.
I couldn't even go to uni now.
I don't much fancy thirty grand of debt.
And that's the point, innit. To scare us off.
They only ever cared for Middle England.
They dropped my mum to win your dad. And then...
They thought we'd just keep coming back for more!

How's it go? You stick a red rosette
on a monkey and they'll vote for it?
Perhaps. But then they stuck one on a fucking
Tory. So fuck 'em, fuck 'em all to hell."

Johnny lit a joint. The room was cold
and everything I'd planned to say was jumbled.
A stumbling, stuttered mess of -ists and -isms
tumbled out: "But we're still... socialists...
They're not! They're just a bunch of racists, Johnny."
"I'm sure some are, but who made you an expert?
Everyone you ever knew was white.
You dickwad. I'm just reading. I'm not squeamish!
I'll read anything! I just want some truth.
But will I vote for UKIP? Probably not.
But they, at least, address the working class
and challenge Brussels. Why do we accept Brussels?
A fucking super-state that business loves?
Romanians all sleeping ten-a-bed
and working shitty eighteen-hour shifts
in Skeggy or some other skuzzy shithole,
sending wages home. Some Worker's Dream!
But when you call it out it they call you racist!
Bleeding-heart, hand-wringing liberal cunts
shaking your cyber-fists from market towns...

You live in London? Yeah, your fucking London.
All sitting on your goldmines up in Bow
and Dalston. Think you're more right-on than me,
extolling social justice from your snugs?
You never had a clue and now you're here...
to save me from myself? Well are you Nick?
You here to save me? What is it you do?
A churnalist. Regurgitating spin
from press releases. Pushing precious pap
from glossy bands in grubby Murdoch mags.
I've read your stuff... I've always read your stuff.
At least you used to mean it. Oh, but now,
well, who can blame you, no one wants a journo.
Money killed your trade, like it killed mine.
You're writing fucking copy Nick, it's bogus.
What happened to your stories, eh? Your novels?
You were gonna write novels, Nick. That's proper."

He had a bloody nerve. "What have you done?
Yes, let's all get a mattress and some Marx!
And shout all over Facebook. I've grown up,
but you just moan. You've pissed your life away.
You were so special. Everybody saw it:
Byron, Michael, Susan, Rachel, Lou.
We idolised you then. You lit our lives.

You were supposed to go and light the world."

Johnny spat. "Too right mate, such injustice!
I know you think I'm playing the vicim, Nick.
But that's just it, I am the fucking victim.
To you it's only ever academic.
I know you get it, mate. But do you feel it?
Have you ever felt it? Does it own you?
Because, I feel it owns me everyday.
That sense that this was always gonna happen.
That you'd become your dad and I'd be... Keith.
They were supposed to change that. They refused!

She died, y'know, me mum... Nah... years ago.
He fucking ground her down. She fucking let him.
I used to hate him... Keith... I used to...
They made us live like animals, stacked up
like that, all misery, squalor and drink.
What chances did he have? A bloke that... shit.
See you're not here to save me, are you Nick?
You came up out of guilt. But this won't cut it.
What did you expect? Quick chat to sort
me out then back to town. That's... charity.
It's like Attlee said... charity's a cruel thing.
Rich men doling out their spare change on

a whim. I won't be fucking calmed down, Nick.
If you don't like to witness all this anger
do something about the shit that makes
us feel that way. If rating Coldplay songs
don't float your boat then go do something else,
DON'T LECTURE ME —
            Well, fine then Nick, I don't
think we can help each other. You should go."
And so, with anger blocking introspection,
I left him in that squalid little room.
A few days later Johnny's profile vanished.

W E'RE GATHERED ON THE REC between the blocks.
On stage, Urbania's tanned CEO
is naming acts. More info packs are handed
round. I look at mine. The ticket prices:
£1400 for weekend pass
and chalet. My God! Fourteen hundred quid!
The crowd around the stage all clap and ooh.
Jonathan Tyle is being eulogised.
And now the time comes to take my notes,
then later type them into postured prose
to flog this thing, this dance on all that pain,
this knowing punchline to a tragedy...
Have you ever felt it? Does it own you?
Much easier to smile and carry on,
write breathy praise for Tyle's latest talk.
It's not so bad. At least I'm comfortable...
Have you ever felt it? Does it own you?
Because I feel it owns me everyday...
Oh fuck it! Fuck 'em, fuck 'em all to hell.
I shut my notebook, ping the band back round
and look up to the roof — the sky is grey
but in my mind it's August dawn,
two stick thin lads sat shooting scorn
way, way up high, the world beneath.
There could be more: more grit, more grief,

more fight. Yes. Yes, there could. I feel it start.
That thump of love and hope back in my heart.